MADELEVA:
ONE WOMAN'S LIFE

Sister M. Madeleva, C.S.C.

MADELEVA:
ONE WOMAN'S LIFE

GAIL PORTER MANDELL

1994 Madeleva Lecture
in Spirituality

PAULIST PRESS
New York/Mahwah

Library of Congress Cataloging-in-Publication Data

Mandell, Gail Porter, 1940-
    Madeleva, one woman's life/Gail Porter Mandell.
        p.   cm.—(Madeleva lecture in spirituality: 1994)
    Includes bibliographical references.
    ISBN 0-8091-3499-3
    1. M. Madeleva (Mary Madeleva), Sister, 1887-1964. 2. Nuns—United States—Biography. I. Title. II. Series.
BX4705.M25663M35   1994
271'.97—dc20   94-5932
[B]   CIP

Published by Paulist Press
997 Macarthur Boulevard
Mahwah, New Jersey 07430

Printed and bound in the
United States of America

*To my mothers and my sisters,
in the flesh and in the spirit.*

ACKNOWLEDGEMENTS

For permission to quote from unpublished materials housed in their archives, I thank Saint Mary's College; the Sisters of the Holy Cross; the Congregation of Holy Cross, Indiana Province; and the University of California at Berkeley. The Sisters of the Holy Cross have also kindly allowed me to quote from the published writings of Sister Madeleva. Special thanks also go to Saint Mary's College and the Knight Foundation for a SISTAR grant, which made it possible for Moira Murphy, a 1992 graduate of Saint Mary's, to collaborate with me during the summer of 1991 on research into the life and times of Sister Madeleva.

Gail Porter Mandell teaches in the Humanistic Studies Program at Saint Mary's College., She received her master's degree from the University of Michigan and her Ph.D. from the University of Notre Dame, both in English. Her publications include *The Phoenix Paradox: A Study of Renewal through Change in the Collected Poems and Last Poems of D.H. Lawrence* (Southern Illinois University Press, 1984) and *Life into Art: Conversations with Seven Contemporary Biographers* (University of Arkansas Press, 1991). She lives in South Bend, Indiana with her husband Daniel.

MADELEVA: ONE WOMAN'S LIFE

INTRODUCTION

Sister Madeleva knew Saint Mary's College as few have: first as a student; then, after she became a member of the Congregation of the Holy Cross, as a teacher and head of the English department; and finally as its third president. Her association with the college spanned almost sixty years, during which she was first shaped by and then became a shaper of its tradition.

As we celebrate the sesquicentennial of Saint Mary's, it seems especially appropriate to recall the life of the woman whose name became synonymous with the college for more than a quarter of a century and whose legacy of wise leadership has proved to be one of its major endowments. Her life and character exemplify the best that Saint Mary's has offered young women for the past 150 years.

For almost seven years, I have devoted much of my own life to researching and writing the life and times of Sister Madeleva. My decision to memorialize her life through biography has puzzled various friends and colleagues. "A nun?" some ask in disbelief. "What can

1

you say about someone who lived in a convent most of her life?"

We live in an age that hungers for stories of women's lives, both private and public, to help us better understand and appreciate female ways of doing things and thus extend our definition of human experience. Madeleva's life as a religious allows us to explore the concept of "vocation" in its fullest significance, as a "calling" to our deepest self as well as to faith and a life's work. Furthermore, her experience in a variety of communities of women allows us to explore examples of female society. Her achievements as a scholar invite us to consider women's intellectual styles. And her long career as a college president and spokesperson for women's education offers us an all too rare model of female leadership. Madeleva's life affords us unaccustomed views from a feminine perspective of American higher education and American Catholicism at crucial times in their history. For that reason alone, her story needs to be told.

Finally, and the point I intend to stress in this talk, Madeleva's talent as a poet and her religious use of that gift enables us to reflect upon a woman's relationship with God, and the intimate connection between creativity and spirituality.

UNLIKELY BEGINNINGS

Viewed with hindsight, Madeleva's life was full of unlikely beginnings. This future nun was the child of a mixed marriage, born to a devout Lutheran father and a militant Catholic mother. She grew up in northern Wisconsin, which at the time was mission territory. Sunday Mass was offered in Cumberland, her hometown, at most once or twice a month. The only Catholic education she received as a child was an occasional Sunday school lesson and whatever her mother taught her from books ordered from Chicago.

This noted scholar and devotee of culture, who earned a doctorate from the University of California at Berkeley and later studied at Oxford, was the daughter of an immigrant, a tradesman who had only a third grade education. She spent her first eighteen years in a rough-hewn logging town of around a thousand inhabitants that boasted no fewer than twenty-four saloons and at least two brothels.

This celebrated educator, with a distinguished teaching and administrative career in private Catholic high schools and colleges for women, was a product of coeducation in public elementary and secondary schools and spent her first year of college at the University of Wisconsin at Madison. There, the future poet and writer, who would publish twelve volumes of poetry as well as scholarly books and scores of essays, began her college career as a mathematics major, one of two females in her algebra and trigonometry classes.

Reading her obituary in *The New York Times*, who would have thought that one woman could attain success in so many different ways—as a poet, a scholar, an educator, and an administrator—any one of which ordinarily requires an entire lifetime? How did "the most renowned nun in the world," as one columnist

3

called her at the time of her death,[1] evolve from such unlikely beginnings?

MADELEVA'S EARLY YEARS

Madeleva was born on May 24, 1887, to August and Lucy Arntz Wolff. They named her Mary Evaline, but called her "Eva" or "Sis." She was the second child of four (the last boy died soon after birth), and the only daughter. Some of her earliest memories were of playing in her father's harness shop with her brothers, Fred and Vern. She loved the outdoors, especially the lake that surrounded the island city of Cumberland. She swam all summer and was the first on skates every winter, with the "ice cracking under every stroke."[2] When her father and brothers went hunting or fishing, she went along. Almost as soon as she could talk, she learned to identify birds, animals, and plants by name.

Eva also learned to garden, keep house, and appreciate good food from her mother, Lucy, a thrifty farmer's daughter who was an excellent housekeeper and cook. Even as a small child, Eva worked in the garden that produced much of the family food; she bore special responsibility for the strawberry and rhubarb patch. Lucy's only extravagance was her love of flowers, which she shared with her young daughter. One of their closest moments came as they silently studied a wild pink moccasin flower they unexpectedly discovered growing out of a rock.

Another of Eva's childhood memories was of sitting

4

on her father's lap while he read to her from his scrapbook of verse. August, who had come to America from his native Germany as a boy of nine, grew up so poor that at age eleven he had to leave school to go to work in a lumber mill. But he loved to draw and to read, especially poetry. Eva traced her love of poetry to their relationship. Thanks to him, poetry for her could never be an act of solitary and silent reading; it must be spoken and heard. She later linked poetry with the Word of John's Gospel. "I love words," she wrote of herself as a poet, "because I love the Word."[3]

Lucy called her children "book and pencil crazy." On her first day in school, Eva could not wait to begin learning. In her autobiography, she tells the story of how she was too eager to get started to wait for directions. With her pencil in her left hand, she copied the first lesson from the board: "The cat is black," starting with the "k" and moving backwards. Her first lesson was a lesson in humility as the teacher invited her to put her chalk in her other hand and start at the other end of the slate and the other side of the sentence. The child must have felt a bit like Alice going through the looking glass.

In many ways, school for Eva was the world on the other side of the glass. In her autobiography, she called that chapter of her life "The Foothills of Parnassus." Books and lessons opened to her mind and imagination the sacred groves of Apollo and the Muses. She mastered mathematics and enjoyed exercising her reason. As an adolescent uncomfortable with ambiguity, she treasured this rich store of right answers. She eagerly learned Latin and read Caesar,

Cicero, and Virgil in the original. Shakespeare, she read for fun. An extravert in spite of her love of books, she chose drama and debate as extracurricular activities, and won the lead in her senior play.

Eva's first attempt at writing poetry came during her last year of high school, when she included her own translations of Goethe's poetry in her senior essay on "German Ballads and Folk Songs." Implicitly, poetry was still linked with her father, whose first language was German, and with spoken (in this case, sung) language.

Eva finished high school at seventeen. She spent a long year at home, waiting until she could join her older brother Fred at the University of Wisconsin. Her father had just built a new shop, and family funds were limited. Fred had worked for a year to save money for school; it was Eva's turn now. Besides, her mother fell ill. Eva did the housework for her mother and most likely clerked in her father's store when he needed help. She spent her free time with her friends, riding in the motor cars and motor boats that made their first appearance in rural Wisconsin. Her mother disapproved, and independent Eva chafed under what she regarded as unnecessary restrictions.

In 1905, few men and even fewer women attended college. That Eva's parents should have permitted their only daughter to leave home, especially when the family needed her help, shows how committed to education they were and how determined she was. Lucy, who had completed high school and taught in a country school for several years before her marriage, had longed for more education. So had August. As a young man, he had worked as an apprentice in Madison, and thought of the university as the epitome of learning. He wanted all his children to go there to school.

Living in a city for the first time, Eva soaked up culture. She went eagerly to concerts and lectures, some in languages she could scarcely understand. She was happy enough with her studies and did well, but something was missing. As she told the story later, one night after a party she sat brushing her long hair in her room in the boarding house where she lived (there was only one dormitory for women on campus). The thought suddenly came to her, "There must be more to life than this. If not, quite logically one should commit suicide."[4]

Although Eva had never heard of Saint Mary's before, she decided to apply after seeing an advertisement in a magazine. Her mother liked the idea that it was a convent school, partly because it was Catholic and partly because she expected it to make a "lady" of her spirited young daughter.

No doubt, part of Saint Mary's appeal for both mother and daughter was that it was a college for women. At that time, coeducation, especially in colleges, was considered to be a dubious experiment. Critics claimed that educating women with men would not only jeopardize the femininity of the women and make them unfit for their primary roles as wives and mothers but would also sap the energy from the intellectual enterprise and rob it of boldness and vigor. The fact remained that the elite educational experiences of the period remained single sex; consequently, many disdained coeducation as not only inferior but vulgar.

As a transfer into Saint Mary's in 1906, when she was nineteen, Eva first distinguished herself by flouting the stringent rules. One crisp fall day soon after her arrival, she cut class to take a walk. The dean, a nun, sent a classmate to find the truant. When asked why she had come to Saint Mary's if she did not intend to observe the rules, she impudently replied that some of the rules were silly. After a year on her own in Madison, Eva found it hard to take seriously the regulations that limited visitors to Wednesday afternoons and mandated chaperones for all trips to town or to the Notre Dame campus. Against the rules, she gave parties in her room and smuggled candy not only into her dorm room but also into the classroom. Her escapades cost her a place on the honors list and in the sodality, but her energy and sense of fun drew her classmates to her.

For the first time, Eva enjoyed the liberating experience of a community designed by and for women, with a brilliant array of female role models. In those days, the brightest and the best women often entered the convent and stayed for life. She idolized one of her teachers, Sister Rita, who was not only talented and beautiful, but good. Under her influence, Eva changed her major to English and began to use her reason to analyze human feelings and try to capture them in poetry and prose.

Assigned by Sister Rita to write a poem, Eva translated another of Goethe's lyrics. Even though she knew that the translation was not very good, the idea of poetry as a translation not just of language but of personal experience into language occurred to her for the first time and excited her. She wrote of the realization: "I had come upon a manner of writing that I had never tried or been taught to use before. The discovery exhilarated me. After that I would lie awake at nights trying to fashion every lovely thing I knew into verse."[5]

Eva, who had grown up without sisters, discovered the power of female friendship at Saint Mary's. She chose, and they chose her, some of the most talented women on campus. They ran the literary society and wrote prize-winning essays and poems (Eva won the privilege of reciting one of hers before an audience at the University of Notre Dame). For fun, they played lawn tennis, paddled around Lake Marian in canoes, had picnics on the island, and, since no males were allowed, danced with each other at their formal balls.

By the light of pink candles, Eva listened as a friend across the hall read aloud to her from the work of the best Catholic poets of their day, Alice Meynell, Francis Thompson, and, their favorite, Coventry Patmore. Eva also read the poetry of Sister Rita, which appeared regularly in the Saint Mary's and Notre Dame literary magazines. Coupled with the retreats required of all students and the prayerful daily environment in which she lived, the poetry began to have its effect. With another friend, she started to attend daily Mass. She enviously watched from afar the groups of novices in the convent gardens. Even though it was always visible, the convent represented a world apart, intriguing and alluring to the young women who lived just

9

beyond its walls. "But God did not make sisters out of girls like me," Eva thought, remembering the cut classes and broken rules.[6]

By the summer following her junior year of college, the young woman knew what she wanted: to become one of the Sisters of the Holy Cross, who then numbered almost a thousand. The image of a society of vigorous, passionate women working together for God and humanity irresistibly attracted the young woman who had once considered suicide as the only rational alternative to a shallow life. Nevertheless, she dreaded telling her family of her decision, especially her Protestant father. When she did, their reaction was even more negative than she had anticipated. The misery of her father almost made her change her mind. On her way to the convent, overcome by her memory of his grief, she wired him to say that if he wanted her to, she would come home.

In fact, still not sure that she would make a good nun, Eva rather expected to be sent home within the first few months. She persevered, however, and her parents, seeing for themselves how happy she was when they traveled to Saint Mary's for her profession of vows, accepted her choice. When he heard her new name, "Sister Mary Madeleva," her father gently teased her, calling her "Model-Eva."

What a later age might consider to be a denial of her identity, Eva Wolff, now Sister Mary Madeleva, regarded as its revelation. The name chosen for her by her superiors pleased her; she interpreted it as "a combination of the names of the mother of God, Magdalen, the friend of Christ, and Eve, the mother of mankind."[7] Here was the full spectrum of feminine experience to identify with. She saw her new life as a religious not as closing off but as opening up possibilities for self-development and self-discovery.

Yes, Madeleva might be sacrificing the possibility of a husband and children to her religious vocation, but so would any woman of her day who chose a career other than marriage. Like others of her time, she accepted the fact that a woman's choice of a career almost certainly entailed celibacy, at least while she pursued her career. In the religious life, she would serve God through meaningful work and enjoy the support of a strong community. Most important of all to her, she would devote her life to loving God and developing a personal relationship with God through Christ.

Not that Madeleva entered the convent with a particular career in mind. She declared herself ready to scrub floors for the rest of her life, if her superiors wished it. She knew that she would have little or no say in what they chose for her. Barely three months after she entered the convent, they made their will known, which both she and they regarded as God's will. She would teach in the academy connected with Saint Mary's.

The day after she learned of her assignment, and with no time to prepare, Madeleva found herself facing her first class of students, most only a few years younger than she. It was an experience she never forgot, and one that would prompt her many years later to become one of the founders of the Sister Formation Movement, dedicated to preventing such situations by ensuring adequate preparation for the work to which sisters were assigned.

Before she had finished her own B.A. degree, Madeleva was teaching college courses. For the next ten years, she taught college English and, as the need arose, various courses in philosophy, French, and theology. During this time, she finished her bachelor's degree and was one of four sisters chosen to begin work on a master's degree at the University of Notre Dame.

Soon after her entry into convent life, Madeleva's superiors cast her as something of a community poet laureate; they requested poems to commemorate feast days and other liturgical occasions. She happily obliged, but also wrote as part of her spiritual life, encouraged by her mistress of novices, Mother Barbara, and by Father Charles O'Donnell, a Holy Cross priest whose poetry was beginning to claim national attention.

Father O'Donnell assigned a sonnet in one of the English classes in which Madeleva was enrolled, immediately recognized her talent, and asked to see everything she had written. With intelligence and sensitivity, he criticized her work, and encouraged her to seek a larger audience. He introduced her to a group of writers, one of whom was Joyce Kilmer. For years afterwards, Father O'Donnell and Madeleva continued to read and criticize each other's work.

The insomnia from which Madeleva chronically suffered proved a blessing during these years. She came to look forward to the silent midnights when she could write without interruption. During the day, walking to and from the classes she taught and the ones she took, she found herself "isolating thoughts, husbanding moments...holding every fraction of quiet for milling these thoughts into lyric form." This process became habitual, and as she put it "almost more secret than my conscience."[8] Her need to write was, in her own words, "imperative." It drove her to exhaustion, until she could do no more. Typically, she then collapsed and went to bed, more and more often into a hospital bed, to recover. And while she lay flat, she composed as furiously as ever.

From her superiors, who had to some extent been prepared by Sister Rita's example to accept and even encourage her writing, Madeleva obtained permission to publish in secular publications and under her religious name instead of anonymously. For a sister to request such permission in the early part of the twentieth century was in itself extraordinary; that her congregation should grant it, and with no apparent fuss or bother, shows how enlightened they were. Madeleva accumulated finished versions of a growing number of the poems that she would publish in her first collection, *Knights Errant* (1923).

In 1919, Madeleva received word of her transfer from Saint Mary's to Ogden, Utah, to serve as principal of Sacred Heart Academy, a high school run by the Holy Cross sisters; she would also teach. The move surprised and disoriented her. She had just completed her M.A., so why would her superiors wish to send her back to high school teaching and administration? Leaving Saint Mary's, her home for the past thirteen years, proved difficult, even though she loved the

13

mountains and found her new community congenial. She accepted the will of her superiors without question, and described herself as in a "thoroughly detached state of mind." But at the same time, she confessed, "I cannot quite find myself spiritually yet."[9]

Madeleva spent the next fourteen years in the West, teaching in Utah and California and, between 1922 and 1925, completing her Ph.D. in English from the University of California at Berkeley. During these years, she established a reputation as a talented young poet and promising scholar. In 1926, she returned from California to Utah, where at the request of the bishop of Salt Lake City, she founded Saint Mary's-of-the-Wasatch (or, more familiarly, "the Wasatch"), one of the few Catholic colleges for women west of the Rockies. As its first dean and president, she laid the foundations of her reputation as an innovative, far-sighted educator and leader.

The Poet and Her Work

Madeleva first distinguished herself as a poet. *Knights Errant*, her first collection of poems, appeared in 1923, shortly after she began her doctoral program at Berkeley. Although many of the poems were recent, written after the move from Indiana to Utah, most had been composed during her first ten years in the convent.

The volume surprised many who thought they knew Madeleva. Her former philosophy teacher and good friend, Father Cornelius Hagerty, C.S.C., wrote her after reading his copy, "I had not taken you seriously as a poet. To be a real poet one must be a great lover. I did not think you were passionate enough to be of the family of Sappho."[10]

In many of these poems, Madeleva invoked an antecedent that suited her own spirit and style: the spiritual vision of nature of Saint Francis of Assisi. Her medieval allusions refer the reader to an earlier tradition that justifies to a modern age her religious themes and archaic diction, much as the writing of her contemporaries Joyce or Yeats counted on mythology to provide a larger context for their personal concerns.

In the medieval setting of the poems, Madeleva's point of view is sometimes startlingly fresh. For example, she gives a voice to the passive object of chivalry: the damsel who is fought for, rescued, served, honored, and secretly loved. In the title poem of the collection, she calls herself, with more than a little irony, "celestial plunder" and complains vigorously to the Lord about the way his supposedly chivalrous knights, Life and Love, treat her: "Life, thou wilt rend this flesh and soul asunder;/ Love, thou wilt break my heart!" Far from docile, the female speaker of other poems in the collection questions her Lord (as in "The Theme"), and takes up her own quest when need be (as in "A Letter to My Most High Lord").

In these poems, written in her twenties, Madeleva spoke emblematically of her relationship with God, a subject that she otherwise rarely addressed publicly, then or later. God is the "King" and the "Most High Lord" served by the "Knights Errant" of her title, a company that includes among others Life, Love, Death, and Saint Francis himself, the "enamored Knight of Calvary." But God as Christ is also her Lover, who in his turn serves her and loves her, body and soul.

In "The Mystic at Table," the female speaker takes up "Water and bread,/ Meager fare spread/ Before my body whence my soul is fed" and in the divine feast that follows is "Awe-fully comforted" as she is "caught up to this,/ Thy breathing bosom, Christ, thy living kiss." When he is not with her, she is miserable, as in "You Sang in My Dream," when she refers to the "numb, inarticulate longing/ Of silent days." But when he is there, as in "The Theme," he reassures her:

> "When, on some ultimate day, in sudden bliss
> I catch thee to My heart in death's fierce kiss,
> I shall have naught to say to thee but this:
> 'I love thee, love thee!'"

As these fragments suggest, the relationship between the female persona of the poems and her lover is tempestuous and ambiguous as well as ecstatic. Her content and language in this and in subsequent volumes of poetry recall that of mystical poets, like Teresa of Avila and John of the Cross, leading some readers to suppose that Madeleva herself may have experienced mystical union with God.

The surviving correspondence between Madeleva and Father Hagerty makes clear that she confided something of her spiritual life to him. He was, as he

16

put it in one of his letters to her, "determined to make a mystic and a poet" out of her.[11] He encouraged her to proclaim her love for God openly, something that went much against her grain.

"You say you love God," he wrote her, "but you do not want anyone to know it. You want to keep it a secret. What about the many American nuns who might learn something of the joys of divine love from you? If God calls you to be his poet, his interpreter to others, then woe to you if you are too ungenerous to let others know your secret."[12]

One can only speculate on what experiences prompted Father Hagerty to guide Madeleva towards a mystical approach to prayer and poetry (which he always speaks of as intimately connected). How far Madeleva went in her exploration of the mysteries of God and religious faith remains unrecorded and, consequently, can only be inferred from the indirect testimony of her writings. That she felt a special affinity for the mystical writers, whom she read avidly during these years, is however a matter of record, as is her often expressed wish during these years that she had entered a contemplative instead of an active order.

Father Hagerty articulated in one of his letters a philosophy of poetry that Madeleva implicitly shared. The true poet, he wrote her, must "have a mind, an intellect, to perceive spiritual reality; secondly...a will intensified by passion to love the vision beheld; thirdly,...imagination to give beautiful body to the purely spiritual ideal."

Madeleva had started down a road whose direction Father Hagerty confirmed, one which he wrote would, if pursued, "lead to sanctity and inspire others to imitate your example." In the sensuous language typical of mystical writing, he advised her: "The more deeply you fall in love with God the Father the more profound and passionate you must become, and hence the more poetical....Love God with the wisdom of Athena, the passion of Venus and the chastity of Diana. Most sisters fear to love lest they become unchaste. In loving God you must have all the passion of the wildest woman with none of her viciousness. The viciousness will soon burn out if you really love God. I congratulate you, then, on not being afraid to love God...I suspect that you have been naked with God and were not ashamed."[13]

More than once in the poems, Madeleva parallels her poetry with prayer (as when she refers in "The Theme" to the talk between the lovers as "The little songs I sing, the prayers I pray"). Poetry and prayer were intimately linked in her experience. In her later years, she was fond of quoting Jacques Maritain's definition of poetry as "the divination of the spiritual in the things of sense." She herself saw poetry as a form of prayer, an understanding to which she came gradually. Early in the 1930s, she wrote her Mother General about her poetry: "You know that I write honestly and sincerely and that it is as much a means of sanctification for me as my prayers. Indeed, much of it is prayer to me."[14]

It seems safe to say that in her early days as a religious, and quite possibly before her decision to enter the convent, Madeleva experienced God in ways difficult to describe in ordinary language. For her the act of writing poetry celebrated and perhaps approximated and even precipitated or sustained that experience. Certainly it shared many of the qualities of prayer, especially prayer of adoration: specifically, certain qualities of contemplation, insight, and self-abandonment.

In Madeleva's mind, far from conflicting with one another, the life of the religious and the artist could, and in her case did, marry—even though it was at times an uneasy alliance. She berated religious communities, including her own, which was more tolerant than most, for undervaluing the artistic gifts of their members. As she wrote a sister religious who was also a talented poet, "I often wonder at the lack of trust we show in these gifts [of God] when they are bestowed within the beautiful security of the cloister."[15]

Insofar as any art form participates in beauty, Madeleva maintained, it is spiritual and can lead beyond itself. She often spoke or wrote of the "apostolate of beauty."[16] Of all God's qualities, she described beauty as the most "irresistible." "Beauty is God's visibility," she said. "We can 'see' it in a way we cannot see Truth or Goodness."[17] Consequently, Madeleva concluded that whether we are believers or not, beauty draws us to God, its ultimate source, more effectively than preaching or proselytizing.

Madeleva conceded that some forms of beauty, and of poetry in particular, reveal God more fully than others. In an essay titled "The Religious Poetry of the Nineteenth Century," collected in *Chaucer's Nuns and Other Essays,* which she published shortly after *Knights Errant,* she distinguished between "the poets whose

19

inspiration was poetry, and the poets whose inspiration was religion," and further divided the latter group into "the poets of doctrine and the poets of personal experience." This second group "sang of intimate union with and experimental knowledge of God." The "soul satisfied by union" who sings—that is Madeleva's definition of the mystical poet.[18]

Madeleva wrote that the mystical poet realizes that "[e]arth, life, the soul, the Church, himself are wedded to God, in a very ecstasy of love. All creation is a multiple mirror, dedicated to the reflection of these unions."[19] About herself, she emphasized that her gift for writing was tied to her religious vocation. She suggested that her poetry began and ended in a relationship initiated by God, not by herself or her own imagination; that indeed her writing flourished only after she entered the convent.[20] The same faith that made her a nun made her a poet.

The responsibility of Madeleva's artistic gifts caused her and her congregation much conflict and anxiety. How much freedom should she have to pursue poetry? Even though her superiors respected her talent and her need to write, the needs of the community often took precedence over the artist's need for time free from other responsibilities. Consequently, even though both she and her superiors regarded her talent as a gift from God that must be used publicly, Madeleva had to find a way to use it on her own, snatching moments as she "walk[ed] through corridors, proctor[ed] study halls, examinations, and recover[ed] from colds."[21]

Most of the poems in *Penelope* (1927), Madeleva's

second collection of verse, were written while she was in California and just after she returned to Utah. She herself deplored the unevenness of its quality;[22] she knew it contained some of the best poems she had yet written but also some that she had passed over for inclusion in her first collection. She even ransacked her college notebooks for some of them. Her publisher had pressured her for a second volume of poems; she had scrambled to produce one in spite of finding it increasingly difficult to write.

Professionally, from 1926 to 1933 Madeleva bore the responsibility for running the Wasatch, including paying off its huge debt. Personally, her relations within her local community in Salt Lake City had become strained to the snapping point. Combined internal and external stress resulted in recurrent physical collapse that often sent her to the hospital and, one summer, home to Wisconsin to recuperate. Her local superior exasperated Madeleva by refusing to take seriously the opinion of her doctor—that some of her duties should be curtailed. Trying to be fair, Madeleva acknowledged her own propensity to imitate Atlas by taking the weight of the world onto her own shoulders. She waged an on-going battle against her tendency to perfectionism and overwork.

Predictably, along with her physical health, Madeleva's interior life suffered, too, although it is difficult to determine what was a symptom and what a cause of her disquiet. She wrote a friend, "I think I told you once that if, knowing religious life and all life as I do now, I could choose again, my decision would be as it is, with the only possible alternative of the

Carmelite convent. More and more one feels the imperative need of the interior life."[23]

Apparently, when Madeleva found it hard to pray, she found it impossible to write poetry. And when she was neither praying nor writing—with real devotion and attention—she found it hard to live well. She wrote to Father O'Donnell, now president of the University of Notre Dame, about her "sense of darkness." He did his best to console her: "Hush, my child, your best songs are coming. Everybody has those times of dark uncertainty. And you can't lose your Dream in any other way than the way one loses one's soul—through one's own doing, which is, of course, misdoing. No, no, be quiet for years, if He wishes it, as He might royally wish it."[24]

The poems that Madeleva wrested from the silence reveal an unsettled spirit. In "Penelope," which William Butler Yeats praised for its passion, the speaker of the poem protests that her condition is far worse than that of the faithful wife of the legendary Odysseus:

> Penelope never has raveled as I have raveled;
> She never has fashioned the fabrics that I have
>   spun;
> And neither her heart nor her lover has traveled as
>   mine has traveled
> Under the sun.

In the poem, she asks, "O Love, how long?" and complains that "loneliness sickens, grief dazes, and doubt pursues me, /With you away."

In this dark time, Madeleva looked to human love and to nature to find God. The poems published in *Penelope* and others that she wrote during these years speak with passion of the embodied love of others and the world. Indeed, some readers, including members of the clergy and of her own congregation, bristled over the sensual quality of the verse. Her superiors fluttered with concern, and even Father O'Donnell questioned her judgment in regard to the spiritual content of some of the work.[25]

Poems such as "The Swimmer" present love, both human and divine, in natural, and explicitly sexual, terms. "The Swimmer," a poem about faith, which Madeleva came to believe justified God's hiddenness,[26] speaks of divine love in terms of its "proxies," in this case, the sea:

Afraid? Of you, strong proxy lover, you God's sea?
I give you my small self ecstatically,
To be caught, held, or buffeted; to rest
Heart to your heart, and breast to breathing breast;
To know on arms and cheeks, on brow and lips the
    bliss,
The stinging madness of one infinite kiss;
Daring your most exquisite, sweet alarms
In the safe compass of the everlasting arms.

Madeleva refused to apologize for the verse that drew fire. She expressly believed that as a religious she should accept and celebrate her sexuality, not deny it. In answer to frequent criticisms, she explained and defended her unconventional view many times

23

throughout her career, as when she wrote: "The love of God for the soul is both virginal and conjugal. Wedded love is a temporal reflection. The fact that its idiom is almost exclusively applied to married love does not disqualify its application to the love between God and the soul. Our surprise at this is an evidence of our obtuseness, I think."[27] She sought guidance conscientiously from her superiors in such matters, but she refused to bow to lesser minds or spirits.

Madeleva lashed out against what she regarded as a Manichean disdain for the body and sexuality that, she felt, corrupted many in the church. She committed herself instead to an ideal of "virginal love," which she described in a letter to her Mother General as able to be shared "without violating the integrity of the lovers." As she explained it, "Our Lady and John knew such love: Christ and Magdalen. It is the one perfect love in the world, and I think that the innocent intimacy of wind and snow, all vitality and all purity, illustrate it. Many of us seem to be Manicheans really, assuming that the body is all evil."[28]

Father Hagerty, who shared a similar view of love and of the body, and in fact encouraged Madeleva in hers, also found himself in hot water. Because of his perceived influence over her, some of her superiors called him on the carpet. He wrote her, "I got some of the blame for your poems. I knew this was inevitable."[29] When he asked for permission to spend the summer at the Wasatch, teaching philosophy and tutoring Madeleva and another nun in mystical theology, Madeleva's superiors curtly refused to grant it. One of the General Council told him, he repeated to

24

Madeleva, that she "should have been confined to good honest prose." He added scathingly, "I suppose she thought that if I spent the summer at St. Mary of the Wasatch more poems might be born."[30]

Eight years separated *Penelope* from *A Question of Lovers,* published in 1935. In the interim, Madeleva resigned as president of the Wasatch, spent a year in Europe, studying at Oxford and traveling through Europe and the Holy Land, and returned to assume the presidency of Saint Mary's. *A Question of Lovers,* included its share of mystical erotica along with a series of poems on Old Testament women that she had written just before she left Utah. Although in her opinion everyone ignored the women in the Bible, she admired what she described as an "unflinching courage that makes the rest of us look aenemic."[31]

One of these, "I Will Remember Rahab," praises the Old Testament prostitute whose generosity and courage saved her. "Rahab was a harlot and lived in Jericho;/ Neither was respectable," the poem begins. And in the same saucy tone, the speaker of the poem concludes: "I remember Rahab to this day,/ And I honor her womanhood for all you say." Lest we forget, the speaker of the poem emphasizes, God's judgment is not the same as ours. For one thing, God is no prude.

The God in these poems is a God of paradoxes, riddles, and mysteries. Enigmatic in their brevity, poems like "Riddles One, Two, and Three" scarcely break the silence. More often than not, their female speakers are taciturn, ironic, and defiant—women without illusions who are nevertheless compelled by a love that has cost them dear. Their lovers have neglected them, failed to appreciate their sacrifices, and sometimes emotionally or physically abandoned them just when they needed love most. This is not young love, tender and easily wounded, but love firmly rooted, able to withstand winter's wounds.

The voice of "Protest Imperative," for example, is the voice of experience; the speaker already knows the answer to her question (she does not even bother with a question mark), but uses it as a chance to challenge her lover:

> Just what would it profit us, were I the oak, you
>   being the wind,
> Would buffet me, torture and shatter me, helpless
>   to bend me to mood of your mind.
> Or were I the pine tree, subduing to music your
>   vagrant unrest,
> You, windwise, would slip the wide noose of my
>   arms, the intricate snare of my breast.
>
> And let us not speak of the grass, prostrate to be
>   trampled by you,
> Scarce lifting its head as you pass to look after the
>   feet it can never pursue.
> Leave off being the wind! I, your lover, have no
>   taste for these:
> The prostrate abjection of grass; the futile, the
>   impotent power of trees.

In this volume, the passionate images of earlier poems—of lovers exchanging glances, embracing, whispering together, feasting, inhaling perfume—while still present, begin to give way to natural images as revelations of divine love. As in "Virgins," wind and trees, stars and mountains express the passions often embodied in earlier poems:

> Though they be lovers, this lithe wind and his clean
>   maid, the snow,
> She has no thought to hold him, nor will he
> Touch with his innocent importunities the white-
>   ness of herself.

In *A Question of Lovers,* death, always present in the poems, steps from the shadows into clear view. The last poem in the collection, "Details for My Burial," was written while Madeleva lay in a hospital in Salt Lake City. At age forty-four, sick and exhausted, she wrote (I quote only the octave of the sonnet):

> As for the matter of my burial,
> It follows hard the golden day I die.
> There needs but a small grave where I may lie,
> Cut in the snow's white peace I love so well,
> Or sweetened with young rain,—one cannot tell—
> But always, always the great, solicitous sky,
> The quick, close earth, and all that live thereby.
> Dear God, how I desire the consecrate cell!

Madeleva playfully showed it to her physician, who assured her that her condition was by no means so dire as all that. The poem infuriated Father Hagerty, who called it pessimistic and life-denying.[32]

Madeleva recovered from that particular illness and continued to write, although she wrote and published less with each passing year. Technically proficient, the later verse generally lacks the fire and daring of the early poems. Like the prima donna past her prime, the songs of the aging poet can still remind one of the old days, but their power comes from the mind and not the moment.

The irony of Madeleva's career as a poet is that her life as a religious explains both why she wrote poetry and why the poetry she wrote wasn't better. Her most original poetry was written just after her profession as a nun and in the early days in Utah and California. That was the period between roughly 1916 and 1926, when she was writing steadily and maturing artistically. The poetry written then gained the interest and respect of a number of contemporary poets and critics, including Harriet Monroe, editor of *Poetry* magazine and mentor to many famous poets in their youth.

As the years passed, the demands of Madeleva's religious vocation, which included her professional vocation as a teacher and, later, an administrator, increasingly absorbed the creative energy it released. On the one hand, she adamantly maintained that she would never have been a poet had she not entered the religious life; on the other, the discipline of that life often undermined the discipline of the poet.

From the beginning of her writing career, Madeleva aimed for a wide audience and consciously avoided religious publishers. She disliked the term "Catholic poet" as inherently limiting, and did her best to define her work in a larger religious tradition that included not only women poets like Christina Rossetti and Emily Dickinson but male poets like George Herbert, Gerard Manley Hopkins, and William Butler Yeats.

Yet Madeleva never made the mistake of denying the wellsprings of her art. In later years, she repeatedly acknowledged the effect on her writing of the Catholic tradition, especially the mystical poets she so loved, and of the female models that both the convent and the college offered her. Without the examples of Sister Rita and of American poet Louise Guiney and English poet Alice Meynell, whose work she discovered at Saint Mary's, Madeleva would never have developed her poetic gifts. Heartened by their examples, she found the courage to explore those areas that touched her most deeply as a woman: her experience of female sexuality as a metaphor for her experience of divine love, and her identification with and interpretation of the experience of legendary and historical women: Penelope, Mary Magdalen, and Rahab, to recall only a few.

However, and here is the irony, the demands of community and professional life and her own diverse talents made sustained poetic achievement difficult for Madeleva. She admitted as much when she wrote in 1950, "The impact of prosaic demands is all but fatal to lyric thinking and expression."[33]

Unfortunately from a purely literary point of view, Madeleva often took short cuts. She rarely revised anything, claiming lack of time (which no doubt was true). She rushed to publish, well aware that the quality of every one of her collections of verse was uneven.

She felt a responsibility to have her poetry pay its own way. Publication tangibly justified the time she spent writing.

In 1926, at a crucial juncture in her artistic development, Harriet Monroe sent Madeleva an insightful critique of her work and suggested a number of revisions that, if taken seriously, could have improved it. For example, she asked for further clarification of the speakers and circumstances of some of the poems, and criticized several as "rhymed prose." Apparently, others were willing to print what Madeleva wrote as she submitted it; in any case, she ignored Monroe's advice.

Madeleva's reputation as a poet grew steadily with the general public long after her most productive days as a poet were past. Increasingly facile, the verse no longer challenged her or her reader. Long periods would pass in which she wrote no poetry at all. Toward the end of her life, Hallmark began buying some of it for greeting cards. Yet, in the late fifties, she carried home major awards from various book clubs and poetry societies in recognition of her achievements as a poet.

But to judge Madeleva on her success or failure as a poet would be to miss the crucial point of both her life and her art. She did not think of herself as a poet in any ordinary sense. "It is a great surprise to me to be considered a poet," she told an interviewer in 1944. "I can never bring myself to talk of myself as a poet."[34] Propelling every poem was a desire to praise God that consciously superseded any urge to create art for its own sake.

This is not to deny that writing loomed large in Madeleva's life, especially in the first half of her long career—it was one of the ways in which she felt most intensely alive. Nor is it to deny that she may at times have cherished visions of greatness as a poet, especially in the wake of her first collection, *Knights Errant*, when distinguished writers and critics anointed her with praise. But in time, Madeleva's spirit found other ways to express itself, more appropriate to changed circumstances, both inner and outer. She relaxed her grasp and let the poetry go—writing until she died, but never with the intensity and passion of her youth. Other work, directed to the same ends, absorbed her as she moved through the middle years into old age.

If Madeleva's poetry has any claim to lasting attention, it is because of its spiritual depth and feminine perspective, which she herself always emphasized as its chief value. In the context of her life, it stands as a testament to one woman's personal covenant with God.

The Scholar

Not only was Madeleva a celebrated poet but also, rare for a woman in her time and certainly for most poets at any time, she held a Ph.D. in English and was a published scholar. The quality of her work at Berkeley, where she produced most of her scholarly writing, prompted her graduate school dean to remark that Madeleva was one of the three best minds then at Berkeley—all of them women.[35]

Madeleva concentrated in medieval literature and

wrote a dissertation on *The Pearl,* a long poem in Middle English. Her book-length *The Pearl: A Study in Spiritual Dryness* was accepted for publication by both the University of California Press and the trade publisher Appleton, under whose imprint it eventually appeared. *The Pearl* was usually interpreted as an elegy, a father's lament for his dead infant daughter; she read it as a spiritual allegory of the religious life. The members of her dissertation committee called her study "distinguished in every way" and commended it as one of the best theses they had ever received.[36]

While Madeleva was still a graduate student, Appleton also published, under the title *Chaucer's Nuns and Other Essays,* critical essays she had written for various classes at Berkeley on the *Canterbury Tales,* the religious poetry of Francis Thompson, nineteenth-century religious poetry, including that of Christina Rossetti and Alice Meynell, and the poetry of Edna St. Vincent Millay.

Madeleva wrote *The Pearl* and four of the five essays collected in *Chaucer's Nuns* while she was commuting three hours each way several times a week between Berkeley and the Holy Cross convent and academy at Woodland, California, where, in addition to serving as principal of the academy and heading the English department, she taught English and French. In spite of such heavy commitments of time and energy, she completed her Ph.D. in record time: just two summer sessions, in 1922 and again in 1923, and one year of part-time followed by one year of full-time work, during which she wrote her dissertation. In consternation, a teacher and friend wrote her, "It fills me with despair, the way you do a day's work at school, write up-holding letters to us needy, make beautiful books, snatch up a degree of the formal sort by the way! But it inspirits me too, the while."[37]

As the first sister and one of very few women at Berkeley to complete requirements for the doctoral degree, Madeleva discovered that she was something of a celebrity. Faculty members and fellow students flocked to her public defense of her dissertation on *The Pearl*. Spectators sat on window ledges and filled the aisles and doorways. Years after the occasion, a witness of the unlikely spectacle of a nun in full habit facing off against a committee of learned men compared her to "a gentle fox surrounded by hounds." "You were mysteriously unafraid," he wrote her.[38] A member of her dissertation committee commented afterwards that she was obviously "sustained by something beyond mere academic competence."[39] Madeleva reassured her Mother General, "One does not lose her Faith necessarily in these places. Teachers and students alike have taken us [sisters] into their hearts as they never do their secular associates."[40]

After she finished her degree, Madeleva had plans for a number of scholarly projects, the most ambitious of which was to trace the continuity of the religious theme through English literature. She also hoped to turn her love of the mystics into a scholarly treatise of some sort. In fact, she found time to do only a translation from Old English for an anthology.

Often, for lack of time, Madeleva had to turn down offers she would have liked to accept. In 1929, four years after her doctoral defense, she wrote her brother, "I have been asked to write a book for the Century Company, but can see only scant opportunity for it."[41] Although she lectured occasionally on Chaucer (for example, she addressed large groups at Columbia University and Catholic University in the summer of 1933) and taught a summer session at Catholic University in 1935, sustained scholarly work ended once she left Berkeley.

Madeleva's responsibilities as dean and president of the Wasatch reduced both her poetry and her research to a trickle, even though her reputation in both areas continued to swell, at least for a while. Even though she fought to make time to read and write, her body—no longer resilient—defeated her.

She hoped a sabbatical year at Oxford would make it possible for her to regain the momentum lost during eight years in college administration (during which she routinely taught several courses each semester plus a full load in summer school). But the year at Oxford produced little scholarly work, in part because of the unexpected illness of her traveling companion, which took her away from her studies from early November until mid-April. She did, however, have the satisfaction of being treated with respect by the dazzling young lecturer C.S. Lewis, who copied out by hand for her his extensive notes for the medieval literature course she took from him during Trinity term.

From Europe, Madeleva wrote to her Mother General that she had just been admitted to the Medieval Academy of Arts and Letters, whose membership included André Maurois, G.K. Chesterton, Hilaire Belloc, and H.G. Wells, and that she was the first woman to be so honored. "Letters are coming from St. Louis and elsewhere asking for lectures, photographs, original manuscripts, etc.," she wrote, adding, "So be prepared to save me from such!"[42]

Madeleva's appeal sounds strange from someone with her academic interests and training. Could she possibly have been sincere in her wish to be "saved" from such requests? Whatever its cause, her attitude raises larger questions: why would she have gone to all the trouble of earning a scholar's degree if not to use it? And why would her religious congregation have allowed her to earn it and then, by overloading her with work, made it virtually impossible for her to use her degree as anything other than a credential?

Immediately clear to anyone who has read Madeleva's scholarly writing in conjunction with her letters and poetry is how entirely she subordinated her intellectual pursuits to spiritual considerations. "I shall be glad to subside into utter obscurity for the rest of my days and expend just half as much energy in learning to know God as I have put on secular subjects this year," she wrote to her Mother General at the end of her graduate work. "If one can work so unremittingly for a degree, one can surely do the same for one's sanctification."[43]

Madeleva seems to have willingly subordinated her scholarly activities, and the worldly ambition that fueled her pleasure in them, to what she regarded as deeper commitments. She had never wanted to be a scholar in order to elucidate literary texts, or to gain knowledge for its own sake. Her letters suggest that she herself regarded the degree as a credential; she bemoaned the American emphasis on advanced degrees and much preferred the "academic sanity" of the British in this regard.[44]

Whenever she could, Madeleva centered her intellectual work on her experience as a religious and used it to further her spiritual development. Far from being detached from or in conflict with her identity as a nun, much of her work as a scholar and critic enabled her to explore areas that interested her intensely and involved her intimately. Her choice of medieval literature as an area of specialization had everything to do with its connection with Catholicism.

In writing *The Pearl,* Madeleva deepened her knowledge of medieval spiritual writing, which in turn enabled her to objectify the difficulties she was experiencing just then in her own relationship with God: her own dark night of the soul. In a difficult time emotionally, her intellect sustained and strengthened her commitment to her vocation. Similarly, her interpretation of Chaucer's Prioress in the essay "Chaucer's Nuns" hinged on her understanding of "chaste and rapturous" love.[45] The essay allowed her to explore in a different context a concept implicit in and essential to her poetry—and, by implication, her relationship with God.

These, however, were just the fringe benefits of an enterprise undertaken in the service of her religious community and in fulfillment of her religious vocation, both of which came first with her. Like Chaucer's Clerk, she would always gladly learn and gladly teach. But returning from Oxford to Saint Mary's in the late summer of 1934, she put her scholarly studies aside once and for all. Her love for things medieval became from that time on an avocation.

Nevertheless, Madeleva's lingering reputation as a scholar won her the respect and friendship of the larger academic community, which she used to good advantage as the president of Saint Mary's College. Today, her scholarly works repay close study less as commentaries on the works themselves (to a generation of post-modernists and deconstructionists, they seem elegant but innocent) than as revelations of her intellectual and spiritual orientation at the time at which she wrote them.

Who knows what sort of scholar Madeleva would have become had she channeled the talent she demonstrated during her brief, brilliant days at Berkeley into a long career? Instead, her life took a different turn, and if she regretted its new direction, she did not sigh for long.

The Educator and Leader

Of her new appointment as president of Saint Mary's, Madeleva wrote to a former professor at Berkeley: "You will consider it quite as much of a disaster as I do, and will yet recognize, as I do, also, that it is not without opportunity."[46]

The unspecified "disaster" to which Madeleva referred was surely the inevitable sacrifice of her poetry and scholarship to the demands of the office of the presidency. From her experience at the Wasatch, she knew the physical, emotional, and spiritual toll that the position would exact from her.

In fact, Madeleva had pleaded with her Mother General not to consider her for the office. Although she had no clear alternative in mind, she seems to have hoped for a less demanding assignment that would have allowed her to teach, pick up the threads of her research, and continue writing the poetry that had started to come again in Europe, along with a rejuvenated prayer life ("I am saying all my prayers, office, spiritual reading with the enthusiasm of a novice and the seclusion of a Carmelite," she wrote her Mother General from Oxford).[47] Instead, two days after her boat docked in Boston, she received the assignment she dreaded. It brought her back to Saint Mary's in the worst years of the depression to shoulder the burden of another college with falling enrollment and a hefty debt.

The "opportunity" that no doubt reconciled Madeleva to such personal and professional sacrifices was the chance to give shape to her own "idea of a university" at the congregation's flagship institution. She found herself "wildly ambitious to recall peripatetic, trivium, and quadrivium curricula. The most intoxicating aspect of the situation," she wrote, "is that I have a faculty who will go all the way with me."[48] Within three months of taking office, she and the faculty were busy rewriting the college catalogue and revising the curriculum in the process. She had already welcomed as visitors to campus poet Louis Untermeyer, Irish storyteller Seumas MacManus, philosophers Etienne Gilson and Jacques Maritain,

English writer Maisie Ward Sheed, and poet Carl Sandburg and his wife.[49]

As the president of Saint Mary's, Madeleva's personal interests and talents and more than half a lifetime of experience came together to transform the college into an innovative, forward-looking institution and to generate positive change in Catholic education and in the Church. In the process, her own sense of herself as a leader was confirmed. "Gradually, I began to see the light," she wrote.[50] Resourceful in her capacity to learn from her mistakes, to think past conventional limits, and to try unlikely combinations, she initiated changes that often seemed like radical departures from tradition but were, in fact, consistent with her own experience and interests. Paradoxically, Madeleva's richest store of innovative ideas came from her love and knowledge of the past, especially the Middle Ages.

Madeleva often expressed her desire to create "another Whitby," first at the Wasatch and then at Saint Mary's. Whitby was a Northumbrian Benedictine monastery where, in the seventh century, learning and the arts flourished under the inspired leadership of a woman, the Abbess of Whitby, Saint Hilda. A scholar herself, she established a noted school at the monastery that educated both women and men, including five future bishops, and augmented the arts. Here, Caedmon, the father of English poetry, crafted his verses; sacred music and art flourished; and scholars, artists, and bishops met in conference. In 664, a synod was convened at Whitby to decide when Easter would be observed in the calendar of the Roman

39

church. Under Hilda's rule, Whitby was a center for both sacred and secular learning, with little distinction between the two.

During the final days of her stay in England, Madeleva traveled as a pilgrim to the little fishing village of Whitby to visit the ruins of the abbey. She carried its image and the ideals of its Abbess back with her to Saint Mary's. In an essay written almost two decades later, Madeleva described the influence of Hilda's example on her own decisions:

"[She] is under my roof, at the very heart of my living and being, this wise, versatile woman, this very Benedictine nun. If there is a problem of building under adverse circumstances, I look at the floor plan of her double monastery at Whitby. If there is a question of educating teachers, she is before me with her best students studying in Rome. If the matter is one of recruiting faculty, I find her drawing on episcopal scholarship from Tarsus to Carthage. As for going to conventions, she was hostess for a synod. Mothering Caedmon, she pioneered workshops of creative writing. She became the mother of English literature. Her universality encompasses me." [51]

Madeleva knew from her own experience that women, even religious women, held second-class citizenship in the Church of her day. She frequently contrasted the respect of non-Catholics for the Sisterhood, which she experienced first at Berkeley and found repeated by her colleagues at the University of Utah, with the condescending attitude of the clergy with whom she came in contact. Many priests refused to regard religious women as represen-

40

tatives of the Church, treating them instead like hand-maidens. One priest became so upset with Madeleva's attitudes and manner, which he regarded as outrageously presumptuous, that he accused her of expecting to be treated like a bishop and reminded her that a priest "is something like a God, and this is as it should be."[52]

Considering the milieu, it comes as no surprise that in the early 1940s, women, including religious women, as well as laymen were barred from the graduate study of theology by all Catholic universities in the United States, in spite of a shortage of teachers. In 1942, the National Catholic Education Association identified this shortage as one of the biggest problems facing Catholic education, and appointed Madeleva to explore possible solutions. Every graduate school she approached, including Catholic University, refused to consider setting up a program for sisters and laypeople. No alternatives seemed to remain. At the next meeting of the NCEA, Madeleva amazed herself by announcing to the group: "I do not know how we will do it, but this summer we will offer at Saint Mary's a six-weeks' graduate program in Theology."[53] Whitby and its Abbess had given her the courage to try.

By the centennial of the college in 1944, the School of Sacred Theology was organized and running. Eighteen sisters registered in the summer of 1943. By the time the School closed almost twenty-five years later, Saint Mary's had granted 76 doctoral and 354 master's degrees in theology to sisters as well as laymen and laywomen. Only after major universities in Europe and America began admitting laypeople did the school phase out its program on which other institutions, like Regina Mundi in Rome, had modelled theirs.

The matter of teacher preparation at all levels and in all subjects was a related concern of Madeleva as an educator. She recalled her own introduction to teaching years before, when totally unprepared she faced her first class of students. In 1948, again through the NCEA, Madeleva proposed a panel to discuss the preparation of religious women for their vocations as teachers. Motivating Madeleva's proposal was her idea of the unity of the religious life, of which both prayer and service were intrinsic aspects. She made no distinction between the religious life of the sister and her ministry, and insisted that professional training should be taken as seriously by each religious community as the spiritual formation of its members.

As a result of the NCEA panel, the Sister Formation Movement came into being. With Madeleva as a consultant, it set up education programs for religious superiors and mistresses of formation who would be responsible for designing and implementing plans to educate their novices. Madeleva designed a program through which a hypothetical "Sister Lucy" could earn her credentials as a teacher while she went through her period as a postulant and novice; she printed it at Saint Mary's as a little brochure called "The Education of Sister Lucy." The college fostered the movement by offering regular summer training sessions, coordinated and administered by Sisters of the Holy Cross.

Madeleva wrote that thanks to the Sister Formation

Movement, "The facts of sister-shortage, sisters' education, sisters' salaries" at last came into the open.[54] Religious women banded together to improve their situation and, consequently, to replace the image of the sister as an "uneducated, immigrant girl" with that of a dedicated professional woman and public representative of the Church. Along with the School of Sacred Theology, the Sister Formation Movement enhanced the status of women in the Church by assuring that they received educations that fit them for roles in the modern world.

Concerned that Saint Mary's have an outstanding faculty, Madeleva convinced her own congregation to send several generations of promising young nuns to graduate programs at outstanding secular universities. Thanks to her intercession, sisters received doctorates from universities that included Yale, Harvard, Columbia, and the University of Chicago; they eventually returned to teach at Saint Mary's with first-rate educations. As she had done years before in her own case, she argued that secular schools need not undermine the faith of a young religious; indeed, as she had seen for herself, a sister's presence at a place like Berkeley or Oxford could enhance the faith of others.

Through the undergraduate curriculum at Saint Mary's, Madeleva found ways to express her knowledge and love of the medieval world. Her encouragement of programs like the Trivium and Christian Culture (now Humanistic Studies) originated in her desire to make Saint Mary's a center of Christian learning, rooted in the Catholic intellectual tradition. The Trivium, a five-hour course required of all students, integrated the study of grammar, logic, and rhetoric (composed of composition and literature). The interdisciplinary Christian Culture major centered the study of western culture on its origins in the Christian past.

Like the Abbess Hilda, Madeleva also devoted herself to establishing a center for the arts. At Saint Mary's, Beauty would find a home. To achieve this end, she brought artists and performers to campus to create their works, stage their plays, and make their music, and eventually built Moreau Hall to serve not only the campus and local community but the entire region of northern Indiana and southern Michigan. In 1956, she arranged for a world premiere of the NBC Opera Company's production of the *Marriage of Figaro* to celebrate the formal opening of O'Laughlin Auditorium, and a few years later, enticed Helen Hayes to campus to act with students in a production of Thornton Wilder's *The Skin of Our Teeth*. She described the steady procession of famous men and women through Saint Mary's as "a progress toward Eternity."[55]

In her administrative style, Madeleva evidenced similarities to an abbess ruling her monastery. Although she instituted faculty and student self-government at the college and depended for advice upon the counsel of her senior officers, she governed hierarchically, assuming autocratic control of most matters of any consequence (as of many inconsequential ones: she proofread every student publication issued by the college).

Madeleva's preferred way of getting things done

was typically one-on-one, in private conferences and meetings. When she focused the power of her personality on an individual, she came close to being irresistible. Her correspondence conveys something of that personal magnetism. Her unique blend of wit, charm, grace, and wisdom overtook those on whom she chose to focus her attention and drew them back to her again and again. As one of her former students put it, "She *chose* people, and made her way in."[56] Poet Louis Untermeyer talked about the experience. She was, he said, "one of the most attractive persons I have ever met. No, I can't say what she looked like. She made us so happy with her. I cannot remember her words, but I know she is kind, witty, and wise."[57]

With increasing consciousness, Madeleva used her office and her personal gifts to foster an educational ideal that encouraged women to use their minds to explore feeling and belief. As she explained her goals in *Conversations with Cassandra,* published in 1961, she wanted to make it possible for "our daughters to think ethically, honestly, morally about civil rights, about segregation, about the sacredness of human life, about power, wealth, truth" (p. 24). She struggled to rectify what she regarded as the "feminine vices: vanity, self-centeredness, self-indulgence, fear of humiliation."[58] Each woman, Madeleva taught, must "battle for personal identity and freedom against the gregarious disease of togetherness." To break through to her deepest self, she will need "courage and a quality of reverence new to her," she wrote.[59]

As the president of a woman's college, Madeleva developed a vocabulary that redefined concepts traditionally and stereotypically associated with women (such as "beauty") and expanded them to include a deeper understanding of the woman as a person in her own right (as when she spoke of a woman's right to receive an education because "she is a person" and thus "obliged to have a beauty of being—apart from hairdos and cosmetics").[60]

Long before psychologists described the differences in a woman's voice and in her preferred ways of knowing, Madeleva asserted that "girls study, learn, and respond to teaching differently from the way boys do, and differently in classes with boys from in groups of girls only. Whatever the reasons for the delicate psychology governing these facts, they are facts."[61]

In Madeleva's development of her own intellectual powers and her insistence that all women cultivate their minds, and through them their spirits, she offered her remedy for improving the lot of her sex. She established a place where women could feel comfortable doing so, and programs to support their efforts. Late in life, she told a reporter, "I do not absolve . . . women on any intellectual level from putting their minds in order, planning for them as they do for their meals, their clothes, their recreations. Their minds deserve even better treatment than their bodies. This they rarely receive."[62] She explicitly included religious women in her call for a richer intellectual life, lamenting in *Conversations with Cassandra* that so many religious are unwilling to think. One of her favorite phrases was, "Just think!"

In the last years of her presidency, which ended in 1961, it is no exaggeration to say that Madeleva had indeed become "the most renowned nun in the world." She had received seven honorary degrees and several major awards, and been invited to give lectures and poetry readings all across the country. In 1957, she lectured in a series on poetry at Boston College that included Robert Frost, Ogden Nash, and T.S. Eliot. That year, *Life* magazine featured a three-page photo-essay on her, and she made an appearance on the forerunner of the *Today* show. In 1959, she published her autobiography, *My First Seventy Years,* which sold so well that it was issued in paperback. Madeleva spent her last years in the spotlight, and Saint Mary's with her.

When she died after surgery on July 25, 1964, at age seventy-seven, hundreds attended her funeral and burial in the convent cemetery behind Saint Mary's. In death, only a simple stone slab bearing her name and dates and the canopy of a flowering tulip tree distinguish her grave from any other.

THE NUN

Ample evidence supports the conclusion that Madeleva's poetry and scholarship fed and was in turn nourished by her religious vocation. Had her career as a college president, so obviously a success when judged by external criteria, also furthered the life of the spirit to which she dedicated herself when she took her vows? Or had Madeleva been a good president at the sacrifice of the rich inner life that characterized her early days in the convent? If so, surely her biographer must regard the undisputed achievements of the last thirty years of her life with sad irony.

The characteristic independence of thought, judgment, and action that spawned Madeleva's achievements as a college president did in fact bring criticism her way, some of it from members of her own congregation. She expected disapproval and disagreement, and took it in stride. "It's friction that keeps the car on the road," she would say, or "We couldn't digest our food at all if a cataract of acid didn't drench it on the way down."[63] Still, she sometimes complained privately in her correspondence to various Mothers General about what she regarded as a lack of understanding and encouragement from others in the community.

Those closest to Madeleva, the members of the Sisters of the Holy Cross, often seemed strangely indifferent to her achievements, perhaps just one more case of the prophet lacking renown in her own land. According to several of her contemporaries in the convent, visitors eagerly sought Madeleva out while many in her own congregation shrugged. One nun expressed her fear that Madeleva's "true worth would not be recognized by our community until we were no longer privileged to have you in our midst." She added ruefully, "There were times when I felt that you would have to die (and even rise again!) to be fully appreciated for your outstanding contribution to Holy Cross."[64]

Criticisms murmured against Madeleva at the Wasatch were amplified through the years at Saint Mary's: that she flouted the rules and used her position to claim selfish perks, like living apart from the community and substituting private meditation for community prayer. That she feigned illness in order to justify such exceptions. That she was inordinately fond of worldly pleasures, like lobster for dinner in the company of cultivated friends.

Envy and small-mindedness no doubt motivated some of these potshots. But Madeleva's unconventionality could also nonplus even the well-intentioned. Never one to bow easily to custom, Madeleva's disregard for convention increased with the years, and with it her reputation for nonconformity. (In Utah, she tied up her skirts and climbed mountains; she whittled and waxed walking sticks as a pastime. At Oxford, she astonished the other American nuns studying there by going about without a companion. When she asked them where she might buy tennis shoes so she could play on the Oxford courts, they didn't know what to think. On a trip home to Cumberland, wanting to swim and having no bathing suit, she borrowed one, even though it happened to be red!) Late in life, she continued to set tongues clucking. She toured Europe for a second time. She spent a week with her friends Clare Boothe Luce and Henry Luce at their Arizona ranch. She traveled to Boston regularly to see her own specialist, stopping to visit friends along the way. Her disregard for customary ways of doing things caused more conservative sorts to regard her with consternation and frequent disapproval.

In her spiritual devotions, Madeleva followed practices that at the time were far from customary, although they may seem unexceptional now. A former student of theology at Saint Mary's, now a contemplative nun, recalls how surprised she was at Madeleva's way of praying. She would pick up a letter, or any object at all, and contemplate it. Other times, perhaps riding in a car, she might suddenly say, "Now let's read some scripture," and then take out a Bible, select a scriptural passage, and meditate on it.[65] Whatever came to hand served a spiritual purpose. Distinctions between "sacred" and "secular" held little meaning for her.[66]

In her friendships, too, Madeleva proved to be something of an exception compared with most religious of her time. Not only within but also outside the community, she formed deep and lasting emotional and intellectual attachments, to both males and females. When she could not see them regularly, she wrote her friends faithfully, in correspondences that lasted in some cases as long as forty years. She went out of her way to visit them and, knowing the importance of small gestures (a poem on a birthday or a book for a special occasion), she took the time and trouble to offer them. She always called herself an extravert; she knew that she required the stimulation of conversation and the consolation of a sympathetic ear. She maintained that love, especially Christian love, is not made at a distance,[67] and so opened herself and drew others close with her gifts of listening and understanding.

Madeleva's poetry and letters support the assessment of a nun who knew her at Oxford: "Sister Madeleva was a 'post-Vatican II nun' without knowing it! She did many things which the rest of us, even the privileged Oxford students, had not yet begun to do!"

As she put it, "She walked alone through the sheltered streets when the rest of us had to find a companion. I was impressed by her quiet charm, her sense of humor, her easy disregard of custom while offending no-one. She never took a stance of independence or of criticism of the *status quo*; she swam through it all with grace."[68] As an entire generation of nuns have done since her death, Madeleva moved out of the strict confines of the convent both figuratively and literally to meet a God hidden but incarnate in the world.

One sees this movement outlined in Madeleva's poems, which supply the fragments of her spiritual and psychological autobiography. Corroborated by the other writings, they offer a glimpse into a woman willing to trust her own experience and to lift her own voice, even when it challenged conventional actions and attitudes, and to use her own creative spirit as a way to God.

What do the poems reveal of Madeleva's inner life in its last phase? And what does the diminishing investment of creative energy in the poetry suggest about Madeleva's interior life and, in particular, her relationship with God? In fact, the later poetry does offer an indication, corroborated by other sources, of how that relationship evolved.

First of all, taken as whole, the poems make clear that Madeleva's relationship with God did in fact change over time—that she experienced God differently at different times in her life. We are used to the idea that our relationships with people change, as choices, emotions, and circumstances dictate. It would seem that during our lives, our image and our experience of God change as we do, if Madeleva's poetry is a valid indication. What may have been appropriate at one stage in our life of faith becomes inappropriate or inadequate later.

In contrast to earlier volumes, the later collections of poems, published as Madeleva moved from mid-life into old age, concern themselves primarily with nature and with the changing seasons, both natural and liturgical. In most of the poems published in the collections that followed *A Question of Lovers,* the speaker looks to nature to find beauty, and in beauty, God. The speaker's outward connection to nature acts as a sign of inward connection to God. A poem like "November Afternoons" (published in *A Song of Bedlam Inn* [1946]) suggests the difference that came with age:

> Now they have come, these afternoons in
>   November,
> When all the air is still and branches are bare,
> And the long, lovely light that I remember
> Invades with luminous peace the untroubled air.
>
> Off to the west a dozen trees together
> Stand in gray loveliness, bemused with light;
> Slender and silver they stand in the autumn
>   weather,
> Waiting the inevitable winter, the inevitable night.
>
> Blossoming light they bear as a single flower,
> And silence more singing-sweet than a lone bird's
>   call.

Off to the west I stand, sharing their hour,
At peace with beauty and needing no song at all.

Madeleva had entered the time of life when familiarity breeds content—when old patterns acquire new significance, repetition renews hope, and the mind restores all things. How many times has the speaker of the poem lived through November? So many that she has become intimately familiar with its particular light, knows as innately as the trees do what comes next, and needs no interpreter. But the moment unfolds unexpectedly, with the "blossoming light," and in it she can see her way past darkness, winter, night, which had once sent her restlessly in search of more tangible comfort.

Madeleva spoke of her perception of passing time in connection with the poem "You Ask My Age" (from *Christmas Eve and Other Poems* [1938]): "I asked myself ...how old am I?; how far back can I think, not remember, but how far back can I think? And I realized that there is no past beyond which I can't. So, I am infinite—potentially infinite and then moving forward I am in the same area of infinity. I can never reach the point beyond which I cannot say, 'Well, after that, what?' So I'm surrounded by two infinites—potentially—although my human existence is going to be finite."[69] For such an understanding of oneself and existence, nature perhaps serves as an apter metaphor for the divine than human form can.

All through her life, nature had been for Madeleva "beauty's self and beauty's giver."[70] Through it, the divine revealed itself in natural epiphanies. The young girl who knew Beaver Dam Lake in all seasons, who tended the strawberry and rhubarb patch in her mother's garden and listened for the first oriole of summer, grew into the woman who debated which she loved more: the mountains or the sea. As a postulant, she shared with the other sisters the gardening tools and seeds her father sent her, and during recreation they worked the Indiana soil. At the Wasatch, in the shadow of the mountain, she used those tools to cultivate her own garden patch.

Back at Saint Mary's, at the height of her career, Madeleva concerned herself with landscaping as well as with curriculum; from her travels, she brought home seeds and cuttings and planted them herself until she found a master gardener who helped her turn her imaginings into gardens. In retirement, she specialized in her favorite flower, the tuberous begonia (with a sideline in pansies and nasturtiums), with which she decorated the college halls and offices. She restored herself by taking long walks "with God," as she told one of her students.[71]

Nature as revelatory of God was a main theme in her poetry, early and late. However, a new approach to nature characterized the later poems. Nature became to her "too mere for metaphors," as she put it in "Old Soldiers"—that is, too pure, too simply itself. As though testing a new realization, the speaker asks the creator of Nature in "Mirrors": "Can I not find you in all winds that blow,/ In the wild loneliness of lark and plover,/ In slender shadow trees upon the snow?" This poem suggests that Madeleva's prayers had gone beyond words; apparently, only silence could express them. If simplicity, in prayer as in life, is a sign of maturing sanctity, then Madeleva's inner life would seem to have deepened through the years.

But what does her movement to God through nature say of relationship? Had Madeleva given up on a personal relationship with God, as a poem like "Mirrors" might suggest? The later poems in fact suggest the opposite. But the image of God and her relationship to God certainly changed. Paradoxically, as she grew older, God grew younger in her verse. No longer personifying God as a father or a lover, as she had in the poems of youth and middle age, the soul of the old poet became a wanderer in search of new life, symbolized forever by the God-child who is born to die and rise again. "We grow young as we approach the source of life," she wrote to Clare Boothe Luce not long before she died.[72]

It may be possible to pinpoint the moment of this particular shift in Madeleva's image of God—an event in her life surely as significant as any of her commencements or awards, but one of those inner happenings that are usually almost impossible to identify and document. It was Christmas eve, 1934, and she was in Hyères, in southern France. The sister with whom she had traveled to Europe had undergone emergency surgery in Paris, where she was studying, and her doctors had recommended that she spend the winter in a warmer climate, to avoid complications. Madeleva left her own studies at Oxford to accompany her. At midnight Mass, Madeleva recorded in her diary "a holy experience, unforgettable." Within the next few days, she wrote a pair of sonnets, "Midnight

55

Mass" and "The Serenade," both of which she collected as "Christmas in Provence." I quote the sestet of
the first of these:

> I had not known that night could be so holy;
> I had not thought that peace could be so deep.
> O passion of night and peace, possess me solely!
> O passion of love, be mine this night to keep!
> O little climbing streets, lead me up slowly
> To where the King I wait for lies asleep!

The King, the secret Lover, who had sought her in
her youth and seemingly abandoned her in mid-life,
once again took her by surprise, defied her expecta-
tions, and amazed her with his faithful love. He
revealed himself anew to her—now, as this newborn
child who had been sleeping peacefully all along and
whose identity with the lover she sought had been hidden from her. As she wrote in "The Serenade," "I
kneel, bemused, song-shaken, weeping,/ A happy-
hearted troubadour in tears."

The crèche she encountered in the church of Saint
Paul in Hyères, entirely local, with regional landmarks
in place of Biblical ones, and Provençal artisans and
peasants instead of shepherds, became for her a sym-
bol of Christ eternally among us. In one of her late
poems, "Parables," Madeleva speaks of all humans as
innkeepers, shepherds, and wise men, who wait for
the Child. If we would find Christ, she implies, we
must learn to identify him in the ordinary and familiar. Christ is coming to birth all around us; we have to
wake up and watch!

To think of God as a Child instead of as a Lover suggests a redirection of both creative and spiritual energy, implying a shift in emphasis from discovery to nurturing. Faith in God's presence, even in so unlikely a form as a helpless baby, moderates the passionate extremes of the ecstasy of union and the anguish over God's hiddenness represented by the relationship between lovers. If we think of our image of God as a representation of our own need for wholeness, it would seem as though the time had come for Madeleva to share in God's role as nurturer and sustainer by recognizing the divine in the small and weak and calling forth her gentler passions.

Madeleva's idea of the sacramental, expressed in her poetry and her personal writings, differed from that held by most of her religious contemporaries. From her reading of the female mystics and her attention to the women in the Bible, she had learned to appreciate the maternal manifestations of the divine well in advance of feminists and to assume an active role in bringing God and humans together.

Madeleva regarded her work at Saint Mary's as this kind of holy work, inspired by Christian love. In classrooms as well as in chapels, in lecture and concert halls, and on paths along the river and through stands of trees and fragrant gardens, she worked to make a place where the young in her care might encounter God through the divine attributes of Beauty, Truth, and Goodness.

All this Madeleva accomplished plagued by chronic ill health, which manifested itself in recurrent attacks of fatigue, dizziness, headache, insomnia, and depression for most of her adult life. Even as a young girl, she had suffered from migraines and insomnia. As she grew older, she often succumbed to severe colds and bronchial infections. Her Boston doctors, whom she began seeing in 1949, when her problems became severe, identified what they referred to as a "considerable liver abnormality" as well as thyroid problems, a very low basal metabolism, and mild diabetes. She struggled during dark moods, when her mind was "like a mud puddle," as she put it,[73] to regard her physical and mental suffering as a route to spiritual perfection.

By doing her work well and bearing her illness with patience and good cheer, Madeleva did her best to serve God in the last years of her long life. At the bidding of her superiors, she had become a Martha instead of the Mary she had perhaps hoped to be. Yet as she pointed out in an essay on the fourteenth-century English contemplative Dame Julian of Norwich, a person might like Julian experience a revelation of divine love only once, but spend the rest of life reliving that "ecstatic union."[74]

Contented with what life had given her, Madeleva formulated a modest credo: "There is always so much to hope for that we must be satisfied with a little less than everything."[75]

CONCLUSION

In many ways, the story of Madeleva's life differs from that of most women of her generation. Its setting was the chapel and work place instead of the home; its emotional center was piety and friendship in place of marriage and the family; and, far different from domestic duties, its routines balanced the spiritual, intellectual and imaginative occupations of the nun, scholar, and poet with the practical responsibilities of the busy executive.

Nor did Madeleva's life parallel that of most men of her time. Although she had achieved a little fame and much success by the end of her life, she did so on her own terms. Rather than confirming the values and achievements of the male world, she directed her energies towards the construction of feminine alternatives in the church and the academy. Thus, she made it possible for women to receive advanced degrees in the previously male realm of theology, and offered young women an education in the arts and sciences that matched that of their brothers in content but differed significantly in approach.

Atypical though it may be in its particulars, Madeleva's life can nevertheless serve as a parable of female existence. Her story discloses that in a convent a woman may find a passageway to the world, and that in a life of apparent limitations—of submission, solitude, and personal poverty—she may create a full and rich life of her own.

NOTES

1. Barbara C. Jencks in *The Providence Visitor.*
2. Sister Madeleva, *My First Seventy Years* (Macmillan, 1959), p. 3. (Hereafter, *MFSY.*)
3. Unpublished biographical statement, Saint Mary's College Archives (hereafter, College Archives).
4. Marjorie Hall Walsh, "Sister Madeleva: Lyric Poet" (unpublished master's thesis submitted to the graduate school of Creighton University, Omaha, Nebraska, January 1962), p. 1.
5. *MFSY,* p.27.
6. *MFSY,* p. 29.
7. *MFSY,* p. 35.
8. *MFSY,* p. 146.
9. Madeleva to Reverend Cornelius Hagerty, C.S.C., Feast of the Ascension [1920?], Indiana Province Archives Center, Notre Dame, Indiana.
10. Hagerty to Madeleva, 9/30/23, College Archives.
11. Hagerty to Madeleva, 6/11/29, College Archives.
12. Hagerty to Madeleva, 10/21/25, College Archives.
13. Hagerty to Madeleva, 9/30/23, College Archives.
14. Madeleva to Mother M. Vincentia Fannon, C.S.C., 10/8/32, College Archives.
15. Madeleva to Sister Mary Francis, P.C., 9/27/46, College Archives.
16. As in Madeleva to Reverend Hilary McDonagh, O.F.M., 7/15/63, College Archives.

17. See Walsh, p. 38.
18. See pp. 92-95 of *Chaucer's Nuns and Other Essays* (Appleton, 1925).
19. *Chaucer's Nuns,* p. 134.
20. Walsh, p. 22.
21. Madeleva to Mrs. N. E. Larsen, 8/11/61, College Archives.
22. Madeleva to Benjamin H. Lehman, 3/7/27, Lehman Papers, the Archives of the University of California at Berkeley.
23. Madeleva to Lehman, 9/15/27, College Archives.
24. Reverend Charles L. O'Donnell, C.S.C., to Madeleva, 11/9/25, College Archives.
25. O'Donnell to Madeleva, 5/19/27, College Archives.
26. See Madeleva to Barbara Ward, 3/26/62, College Archives.
27. Madeleva to Reverend Bonaventure Schwinn, 6/24/55, College Archives.
28. Madeleva to Vincentia, 10/8/32, College Archives.
29. Hagerty to Madeleva, 1/16/29, College Archives.
30. Hagerty to Madeleva, 6/11/29, College Archives.
31. Madeleva to Vincentia, 10/8/32, College Archives.
32. Hagerty to Madeleva, 9/11/31, College Archives.
33. Madeleva to G. Bromley Oxnam, 6/6/50, College Archives.
34. *Catholic Poetry Society of America Bulletin,* February 1944.
35. Sister M. Mercedes, O.P. to Sister Conception, 3/28/25, College Archives, quoting Dean Lipman of Berkeley, who had spoken with her about Sister Madeleva. Madeleva was temporarily living in the Dominican convent in Oakland at the time.
36. Madeleva to Mother M. Aquina Kerwin, C.S.C., Easter 1925, General Archives of the Sisters of the Holy Cross (hereafter, General Archives).

37. Lehman to Madeleva, undated (probably late 1925 or early 1926)), College Archives.
38. Vernon Patterson to Madeleva, 4/20/64, College Archives.
39. *MFSY*, p. 54.
40. Madeleva to Aquina, Easter, 1925, General Archives.
41. Madeleva to J. Frederick Wolff, Easter Sunday 1929, private collection.
42. Madeleva to Vincentia, Feast of Apparition of Saint Michael 1934, General Archives.
43. Madeleva to Aquina, Easter 1925, General Archives.
44. Madeleva to Vincentia, 10/21/33, General Archives.
45. See p. 41 of *Chaucer's Nuns*.
46. Madeleva to Lehman, 1/2/35, Lehman Papers.
47. Madeleva to Vincentia, 10/21/33, College Archives.
48. Madeleva to Lehman, 1/2/35, Lehman Papers.
49. Madeleva to Lehman, 1/2/35, Lehman Papers.
50. *MFSY*, p. 95.
51. From a manuscript, College Archives, later published as "Saint Hilda of Whitby" in *Saints for Now*, ed. by Clare Boothe Luce (Sheed and Ward, 1952).
52. Reverend John R. McCarthy in the *Steubenville Register*, 3/27/59.
53. *MFSY*, p. 115.
54. *MFSY*, p. 113.
55. Madeleva to Lehman, 10/22/35, Lehman Papers.
56. Interview with Sister Mary of God, O.P.
57. Jean Starr Untermeyer to Madeleva, 5/8/31, College Archives.
58. Madeleva to Martha Blocker, 8/27/60, College Archives.
59. *Conversations with Cassandra* (Macmillan, 1961), p. 19.
60. Interview in the *Montreal Gazette*, 6/23/62.
61. *MFSY*, pp.128-129.
62. Interview in the *Milwaukee Journal*, Thursday, 4/18/63.

63. Sister Mary Immaculate Creek, C.S.C., *A Panorama: 1844-1977* (Saint Mary's College, 1977), p. 130.
64. Sister Gerald Hartney, C.S.C., to Madeleva, 5/22/62, College Archives.
65. Interview with Mary of God.
66. See, for example, her comments in *MFSY*, p. 137, on the "literally and holily secular."
67. Walsh, p. 130.
68. Mother Margaret Williams, R.S.C.J., to Gail Mandell, 5/3/88.
69. Walsh, p. 60.
70. *MFSY*, p. 12.
71. See Walsh, p. 34.
72. Madeleva to Clare Boothe Luce, 5/7/62, College Archives.
73. Madeleva to Dr. John W. Norcross, M. D., of the Leahy Clinic in Boston, 3/8/50, College Archives.
74. *Conversations with Cassandra,* p. 130.
75. Madeleva to Sister Mary Patrick, I.H.M., 6/30/52, College Archives.

PUBLISHED WORKS OF SISTER MADELEVA CITED IN THIS LECTURE

Knights Errant and Other Poems. D. Appleton, 1923.

Chaucer's Nuns and Other Essays. D. Appleton, 1925.

The Pearl: A Study in Spiritual Dryness. D. Appleton, 1925.

Penelope and Other Poems. D. Appleton, 1927.

A Question of Lovers and Other Poems. Saint Anthony Guild Press, 1935.

Christmas Eve and Other Poems. Saint Anthony Guild Press, 1938.

A Song of Bedlam Inn. Saint Anthony Guild Press, 1946.

My First Seventy Years. Macmillan, 1959.

Conversations with Cassandra. Macmillan, 1961.

The Madeleva Lecture in Spirituality

This series, sponsored by the Center for Spirituality, Saint Mary's College, Notre Dame, Indiana, honors annually the woman who as president of the college inaugurated its pioneering program in theology, Sister M. Madeleva, C.S.C.

1985
Monika K. Hellwig
Christian Women in a Troubled World

1986
Sandra M. Schneiders
Women and the Word

1987
Mary Collins
Women at Prayer

1988
Maria Harris
Women and Teaching

1989
Elizabeth Dreyer
Passionate Women: Two Medieval Mystics

1990
Joan Chittister
Job's Daughters

1991
Dolores R. Leckey
Women and Creativity

1992
Lisa Sowle Cahill
Women and Sexuality

1993
Elizabeth A. Johnson
Women, Earth and Creator Spirit